FROM ABBEVILLE TO ZEBULON

GITY DRUG CO. W.A.CHERRY, OPTICIAN.

Depot St. looking north. Abbeville, Ga. 3484

Pub by Art Novelty Pub Co.

Street Scene

ZEBULON, GA.

BANK

FROM ABBEVILLE TO ZEBULON

EARLY POST CARD VIEWS OF GEORGIA

EDITED BY

GARY L. DOSTER

THE UNIVERSITY OF GEORGIA PRESS   ATHENS AND LONDON

© 1991 by the University of Georgia Press
Athens, Georgia 30602
All rights reserved

The post cards are reproduced at 86% to 96% of original size.
Hand-lettering by James Stacy
Set in Century Old Style by G&S Typesetters
Printed and bound by Thomson-Shore
The paper in this book meets the guidelines for permanence and
durability of the Committee on Production Guidelines for
Book Longevity of the Council on Library Resources.

Printed in the United States of America
95 94 93 92 91   C   5 4 3 2 1

Library of Congress Cataloging in Publication Data

From Abbeville to Zebulon : early post card views of Georgia /
edited by Gary L. Doster.
p.   cm.
Includes index.
ISBN 0-8203-1334-3 (alk. paper)
1. Georgia—Description and travel—
Views.   2. Postcards—Georgia.
I. Doster, Gary L.
F287.F76 1991
917.5804′43—dc20   90-27741
CIP

British Library Cataloging in Publication Data available

To Faye Thomas Doster
My Sweetheart, Friend, and Wife
for More than Thirty Years

CONTENTS

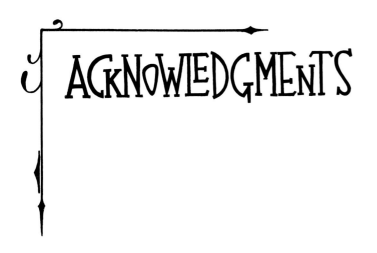

ACKNOWLEDGMENTS

During the preparation of this book I became indebted to a large number of friends and associates who were eager to help in many ways. To each of them I extend my sincere gratitude. If someone has inadvertently been overlooked, please forgive me.

Charles East, Larry Gulley, and Shelia Hackney were responsible for my undertaking the project in the first place. Their gentle prodding and encouragement finally prompted me to get started. In the early stages I received valuable advice and suggestions from Doug Clark, Jennie Johnson, Sue Fan Tate, and Lonnie Williamson. Once the book was underway Charles East took a personal interest in its development and invested a great deal of effort in seeing it through to completion. His expert editing skills were greatly appreciated.

Karen Orchard and Sandra Strother Hudson of the University of Georgia Press could not have been more delightful to work with. Their expertise and input were vital during every phase of the production of the book, and they contributed many ideas and suggestions that improved on my efforts considerably.

Some good friends and fellow post card collectors who provided aid and assistance along the way were Carl Anderson, "H" Armor, Bob Basford, Steve and Eleanor Blackmon, Ted Brooke, Pete Brown, Steve and Rebecca Gurr, John Kovalski, Bucky Redwine, Gordon Sanford, John Shriner, Phinizy Spalding, Bill Walsh, Jeff West, and Les Winn. Several professional post card dealers (also good friends) who have been especially helpful through the years in providing good Georgia cards for my collection include J. C. Ballentine, John Gibbs, John Gingerich, Myrta Hall, Frank Howard, Fred Kahn, Jack Leach, Michael Leach, Ernest Malcom, Charlie McCoy, Vickie Prater, Jim Petit, Jr., and Herbert Schulman. I am particularly grateful to Ernest Malcom for the opportunity to acquire so many wonderful cards from the Albertype collection.

For her lifetime of generosity and patience, I offer my thanks and love to my wife, Faye.

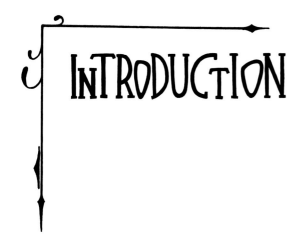

INTRODUCTION

Just after entering the twentieth century, the United States was swept up in the worldwide craze of post card collecting that had begun in Europe several years earlier. What had started as a cheap, convenient form of communication soon evolved into a popular pastime for nearly everyone. Collectors traded cards from town to town, from state to state, and eventually from country to country. Post card collecting reached almost fanatical proportions, and the cards were sometimes bought and exchanged under unusual and even amusing circumstances. For example, when rural folk, who comprised the vast majority of the population at that time, went into town for weekly or monthly provisions, they might mail cards back home to friends, other family members, or even to themselves. The cards would arrive the day after—or the day after the day after—they returned home!

In the larger towns, and in many of the smaller towns as well, the cards were sold in drugstores, and indeed the town drugstore was frequently the publisher or the sponsor of the views. This no doubt explains why so many of these stores are seen in the views of main streets and business sections: the post card was, or could be, an inexpensive means of advertising. The post cards could also be found in stationery stores and bookstores as well as in hotels and railroad stations. Those passing through the state by rail might leave the train during its stop in Macon or Atlanta to buy and mail cards to family at home or to fellow collectors. Cards postmarked in the city that was the subject of the view were particularly sought after. There were collectors who specialized and who might collect nothing except views of depots and railroad terminals. Others collected main streets or courthouses or state capitols.

Cards were collected, traded, stored away in boxes, and displayed in fancy albums that oftentimes lay alongside the family Bible on the parlor table. There were even wooden hearth screens that held cards—the perfect addition to the already crowded Edwardian parlor. The hobby became so popular that in 1909 one national post card collector's club based in Philadelphia boasted of having ten thousand members. In Europe, where it had all started, Queen Victoria became enamored of the hobby and had a member of her family establish a collection for her.

The history of picture post cards goes back to the 1860s and the appearance of the first "postal cards," which were issued by a government agency and had the postage stamp imprinted on them. "Post cards," on the other hand, were privately produced, with the postage stamp affixed by the sender. There had been a few early attempts to promote privately produced post cards outside of Europe, but all had failed. Such cards were printed for a short time in the United States by J. P. Charlton and H. L. Lipman of Philadelphia. Copyrighted by Charlton on December 17, 1861, and published by Lipman, their private "postal card" never caught on. The first government-issued postal card was introduced in Austria in 1869. One side was reserved for the address and the other provided space for a short message. Public response was overwhelming. The governments of England, Germany, and Switzerland began issuing postal cards in 1870, and more than a dozen other countries followed within the next five years, including Canada in 1871 and the United States two years later. Over sixty million of the United States government issues of 1873 (fig. 1) were sold within six months. Widespread publication of private post cards was yet to come, however.

The U.S. Post Office Department had anticipated that the postal cards would be used for "orders, invitations, notices, receipts, acknowledgments, price lists, and other requirements of business and social life," and many businesses seized the opportunity to use the cards for

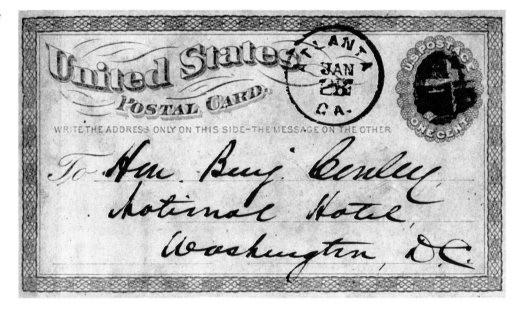

Figure 1. The one-cent rate imprinted on the first government-issued postal card of 1873 remained constant until 1917, when it was increased to two cents. Two years later the one-cent rate was reinstated. Not until 1951 was there to be another rate increase on postal cards issued by the government.

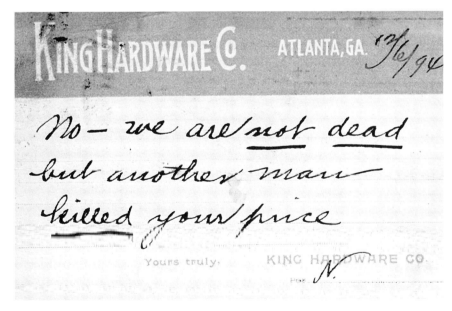

Figure 2. An example of the early use of a U.S. postal card for advertising.

advertising (fig. 2). One interesting use to which the cards were put occurred in Baker County, Georgia, where the warden of the prison there used them to inform other law enforcement officers across the state of the escape of prisoners (fig. 3). Some individuals took it upon themselves to embellish the government-issued cards with decorative symbols and figures to make them more attractive. There are even some examples of this practice in the United States (fig. 4). From this beginning, the picture post card eventually evolved.

As early as 1870, small designs were added to some of the postal cards, and in 1872 a card was produced in Vienna that had an illustration that occupied the entire address side of the card. The first real picture post cards available in quantity for public use were printed by a Paris newspaper in conjunction with the Exposition Universelle in Paris in 1889. The cards were illustrated with a black and white vignette of the Eiffel Tower completed earlier that year and were sold at the base of the tower as mementos of the occasion. This event was probably the inspiration for the production of the first picture post cards in the United States—souvenirs of the World Columbian Exposition held in Chicago in 1893 (fig. 5)—though the idea may also have come from a set of souvenir pictures of similar size that were sold at the 1876 Centennial Exposition in Philadelphia. The Philadelphia views were not designed to be post cards, however. The beautifully colored views of the Chicago exposition

Rewards for the Follwing Convicts.

Who escaped the first of June, 1918, from Baker County, Ga.

$50 Reward for the Capture and Return of James Pattersaul, Color black, Age 33, Height 5ft 9in, Weight 135 lbs., black hair and eyes. Has two scars from shot above left knee. Both thighs have been broken. Very bowleged, Fair education. Has big pop eyes.

$50 Reward for Capture and return of Ben Smith, white, age 40, height 5ft 7 in., weight 150lbs, brown hair, blue eyes. Had heavy mustache when he escaped.

$50 Reward for the Capture and Return of Melvin McGown, color dark brown, age 35, height 5ft, 10 1-2 in., weight 170 lbs, had heavy black mustache when he escaped.

$50 Reward for Capture and Return of Peck Myrick, color dark brown, age 28, height 5ft 11 in. Weight 180 lbs., black hair and eyes. Notify EDGE ANDREWS, Warden, Newton, Ga.

Figure 3. The prison warden in Baker County, Georgia, used a U.S. postal card to notify law enforcement officers across the state of the escape of prisoners.

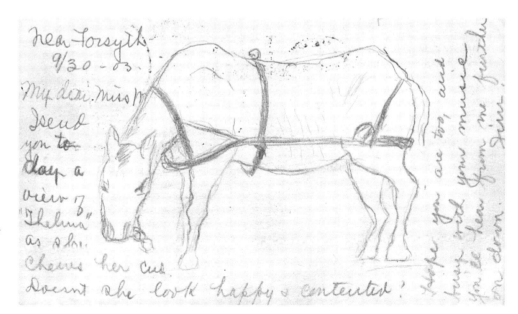

Figure 4. A homemade post card drawn on a U.S. issue was mailed from Forsyth, Georgia, to Athens, Georgia, September 30, 1903.

proved to be extremely popular and helped lead the way to the passage of an 1898 law permitting "Private Mailing Cards" with the same one-cent postage rate and mailing privileges as government issues (fig. 6).

After the success of the Columbian Exposition issues, several companies began limited production of views of larger towns in the late 1890s. This merely whetted the public's appetite for such cards. Commercial companies, large and small, as well as private entrepreneurs began a great rush to supply the demand (fig. 7). In 1902 the Eastman Kodak Company contributed greatly to the movement when it introduced postcard-size paper on which photographs could be printed directly from negatives. This idea was soon duplicated by several Kodak competitors and the product was distributed widely. Subsequent improvements in the process enabled amateurs to produce their own post cards (figs. 8, 9).

Most of the post cards from the early 1900s, however, are color lithographs that were printed in Europe, many of the best of them produced in Germany. The process frequently involved painstaking work with as many as seven or eight or even ten different lithographic stones—one for each shade or color, which explains the delicate coloring to be found in the best of them. Some of the cards from this period were printed in black and white and then colored by hand. Because these printed views are not actual photographs, but color reproductions of photographs, they have too often been undervalued or

Figure 5. Design number eight of a set of ten cards issued in 1893 commemorating the World Columbian Exposition held in Chicago.

Figure 6. The Private Mailing Card authorized by Act of Congress May 19, 1898, legalized the use of privately produced post cards and permitted them the same one-cent rate as government postal cards.

Figure 7. A 1905 ad offering the services of one of the earliest and largest producers of post cards in the U.S.

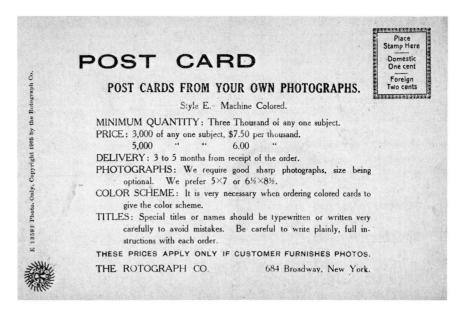

Figure 8. This homemade real photograph card depicts a tranquil scene in Bowman, Georgia, in 1909.

Figure 9. Another real photograph card portrays Gordon Sanford and friends at home at 975 Oglethorpe Avenue, Athens, Ga., circa 1913.

even dismissed as ephemera. Those who downplay the cards overlook the fact that they began as photographs and serve much the same purpose—and that with the passage of time they have become historical documents. All too often, the photographs from which the lithographs were made have been lost. But the cards survive because they were produced in large numbers.

The cards tell us a great deal more than what the town's first post office looked like, or the school long since gone, or the courthouse that burned in 1907. They are an index to the town's attitudes and social values—to its view of itself. What did it consider important? Did it concern itself only with the "progress" that was given such emphasis in the early years of the century, or were there moments of contemplation and reflection? And what were the individuals who sent these post cards saying to each other?

One of the attractions of the cards of course was that there was very little space in which to write and thus the purpose of a letter could be served in a few short sentences or phrases. During the early years, one side of the card was reserved for the address only, which meant that messages had to be written on the picture side of the card. This explains why so many early cards were defaced by the sender (fig. 10). A 1907 law allowed the use of a "divided back," so that the address and the message could be placed on the same side (fig. 11). Because of the limited space, a kind of post card shorthand developed: "Having grand time," "Used to have a girl here," "Arrived this eve," "Roads near impossible." No longer was it necessary to start a sentence in the customary way, or even to complete one. Spelling fell by the wayside. "Staid here last nite," "Hello Rosanelle—if your name is not spelt right I can't help it." The people who scrawled these notes seem to have been in a hurry. "In a few days we will be at home if we don't run the wheels off," wrote one of the senders. The quotations that begin each of the sections suggest the flavor of these messages.

While 1898 to 1918 is considered to be the period of greatest popularity for picture post cards worldwide, the American golden age of these cards was from 1905 to 1915. It was during this decade that photography and printing reached a point of excellence that permitted the production of high-quality cards that could be mass-produced cheaply. As important, the Rural Free Delivery

system devised by the U.S. Post Office Department in 1898 came into its own. Until then, only 25 percent of U.S. citizens lived in towns with populations of ten thousand or more, which made them eligible for home mail delivery. Those living in smaller towns had to retrieve their mail at the post office, and those living in the country had to make periodic trips into the nearest town to get theirs. Now, by petitioning their congressmen, rural residents could receive the same service as their big-city friends. By the early 1900s, all but the most remote households could enjoy mail deliveries right to their doors.

After 1915 the collection fad declined and so did the quality of the cards, in part a victim of World War I, which cut off access to Germany and the German printers who had produced so many of the views. But the rise of the telephone and the automobile were also contributing factors. With the coming of the second decade of the twentieth century, the telephone became less a luxury item than a common household fixture, thereby reducing the value of the post card as a convenient form of communication. Then too, as more people acquired automobiles, distances narrowed and the need to stay in touch by mail was much less compelling. Post cards would continue to be produced, but they had lost much of their original purpose.

The first picture post cards from Georgia were a set of twelve views commemorating the Cotton States Exposition held in Atlanta in 1895 and sold from vending machines at the exposition (fig. 12). After this event a few black and white views of Savannah and Atlanta were published (fig. 13), but it was not until after the turn of the century that post card views of other Georgia towns were produced. By then the great fad that was already raging in Europe spilled over to the United States, and Georgia was soon as infatuated with post card collecting as the rest of the country.

We are fortunate that Georgians became infected with the "post card fever," for in the effort to satisfy the demand for more cards almost any scene was fair game for the post card manufacturers. Thus, scenes never photographed before were captured on film and reproduced on post cards, and we are richer historically for them. Many of these cards represent the only surviving record of churches, schools, homes, business establishments, and public buildings long ago demolished or destroyed by fire

Figure 10. Because it was illegal to write anything but the address on the back of pre-1907 U.S. post cards, messages were often written across the face of the card.

VIEW ON LOVE AVENUE
TIFTON, GEORGIA

Figure 11. After 1907 it was legal to write a message on the same side of the post card as the address. A line was printed down the middle of the card, dividing the space allotted for each.

Figure 12. One of the cards from the set of twelve produced to commemorate the 1895 Cotton States Exposition in Atlanta.

Even events such as storms, fires, dedications, and re-unions—especially reunions of Confederate veterans—are recorded.

Where else would one find a photograph of seventeen friends gathered for Ruth Glasier's house party at Flat Shoals, Georgia, on August 3, 1908? Or get a look at mule-drawn streetcars plying the dirt streets of Covington, Oxford, and Washington, Georgia, early in the century? Or see a picture of a lazy scene in Adel, Georgia, in 1910 with a pig walking down the dirt main street? The value of these views to anyone interested in the history and culture of the state is obvious.

Figure 13. An early black and white view of Atlanta produced by the Albertype Company of New York.

FROM ABBEVILLE TO ZEBULON

BIRD'S-EYE VIEWS

*"You can just imagine the size of this town—
but nice people."*

Bird's-eye views were among the most popular of the picture post cards produced in the early years of the century. Photographers climbed to the roofs of the tallest buildings in town, an upper floor or the dome of the courthouse or city hall, or the belfry of one of the churches. Sometimes the photographer aimed his camera out of a hotel window (for instance, Stuart's Hotel in Thomasville), or from the window of his own gallery. In the cities the buildings were taller and therefore the views were frequently taken from a higher elevation, like those photographed from the Georgia State Life Insurance Company

Building in Macon or the Flatiron Building in Atlanta.

The wonder is that views of so many of the small towns were taken, and that the collection and exchange of post cards preserved them. What we see, across the rooftops of stores and residences, are Georgia towns that superficially differed very little from one to another. There are the blocks of buildings that comprised the business section. The homes are usually large and of frame construction—and may not be representative, since towns were in the business of putting their best foot forward. Sometimes the streets are deserted, or nearly so, for that of course was the way these streets often were, but also because the photographer was afraid to risk the blur of movement. The poles strung with electric wires anticipate the progress to come, but at the same time intrude on a scene marked by shade trees and picket fences.

Bird's Eye View, Savannah, Ga.

Birdseye View, Valdosta, Ga., Looking North From Court House.

Birds Eye View, Albany, Ga.

View from Top of Windsor Hotel looking South-East, Americus, Ga.

ARLINGTON, GA.   General View business Section

4

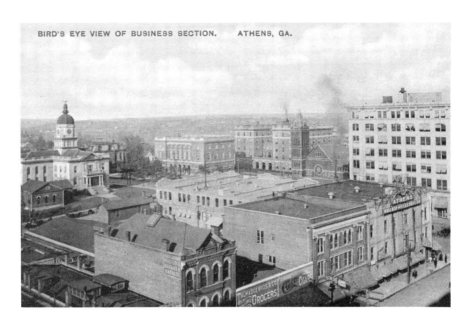

BIRD'S EYE VIEW OF BUSINESS SECTION.   ATHENS, GA.

Bird's-eye View of Atlanta showing Peachtree Street, Atlanta, Ga.

Birds Eye View of Augusta, Ga.

5

Birdseye View of Barnesville, Ga.

BIRDS EYE VIEW. BLUE RIDGE, GA.

Butler Island
Plantation, Ga.
Former home of
Fanny Kemble

Our little town is a lot prettier than it shows up in this picture. "Miss Jessie".

PARTIAL BIRDS-EYE VIEW, CARROLLTON, GA.

CEDARTOWN, GA.   Bird's Eye View

Birdseye View Colquitt, Ga., Northwest from Court House

A 13542 GENERAL VIEW, COLUMBUS, GA.

The City, so-called—I enjoyed your postal
6/16/06 —very much. look natural. B

Birdseye View, Commerce Ga., Looking South. July 2nd 9,'09

You can just imagine the
size of this town — but nice
people—love Mae 10/27/09

Looking Northeast from Court House Dome, Cordele, Ga.

DAWSON, GA.   Bird's Eye View

DOUBLE KNOBS   1922.
Looking East

BIRD'S-EYE VIEW OF ELBERTON, GA.

Elberton is a very nice little town
of 6,500 inhabitants
Harry

Bird's Eye View of Fitzgerald Ga.

BIRD'S-EYE VIEW OF FORT VALLEY, GA., LOOKING NORTH.

Birdseye View Brenau College Conservatory, Gainesville, Ga.

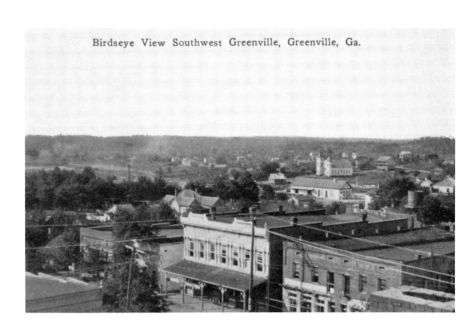

Birdseye View Southwest Greenville, Greenville, Ga.

Bird's Eye View of Griffin, Ga.

Birdseye View Hawkinsville, Ga.

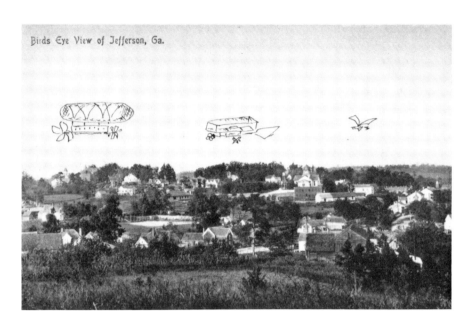

Birds Eye View of Jefferson, Ga.

Bird's Eye View looking East, McDonough, Ga.

Bird's-eye View, Nashville, Ga.

Birds-eye View. QUITMAN, Ga.

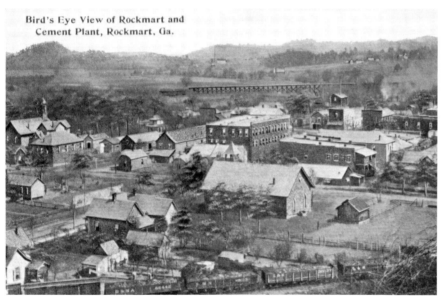

Bird's Eye View of Rockmart and
Cement Plant, Rockmart, Ga.

BIRDSEYE VIEW
OF ROME, GA.

Arthur Livingston, Publisher, New York 943

13

SAVANNAH HARBOR LOOKING WEST, SAVANNAH, GA.

Bull St. South, Savannah, Ga.—Moonlight.

Birdseye view of Tallapoosa, Ga.

Bird's Eye View from Stuart's Hotel, Thomasville, Ga.

Tybee Island, Ga. View from Hotel Tybee.

Bird's Eye View Business Section West, Vidalia, Ga.   18568

15

MAIN STREETS AND TOWN SQUARES

*"This is the street papa's store is on,
but you can't see it in the picture."*

It was on their main streets and courthouse squares that the towns did their business. In the early years of the century the typical Georgia town was a predictable mix of "fancy grocers," general merchandise stores, drugstores, dry goods stores, hardware stores (which usually sold farm implements), stores that sold feed and seed, and millinery shops that attracted women customers. Every town had a bank, and many had two, and somewhere along Main Street or on one of the streets fronting the square were the post office and a Western Union office.

If the courthouse square was a center of the town's business activity, it was also the place where the men of

Peachtree Street Looking, South, Atlanta, Ga.

the town and county gathered, especially when court was in session. Here farmers came to talk not only about the trial underway inside but also about crops and the weather. Merchants and business people might be seen here too, though more often they stood in their doorways and exchanged the small talk of the day when they were not with their customers. The townspeople are in fact one of the most interesting aspects of the visual record these post card views provide us, as they stand in the middle of the street or strung out along the row of stores looking into the camera. Here, frozen in a moment of time, are some of the men of the town posed in front of

Paulk's Drug Store in Alapaha, a group of citizens gathered on Main Street in Fort Valley, and another congregated on the west side of the square in Dallas. "Do you recognize 'Uncle Jake' on this picture?" asks the sender.

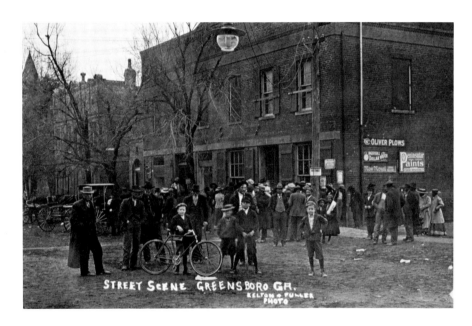

STREET SCENE GREENSBORO GA.
KELTON & FULLER PHOTO

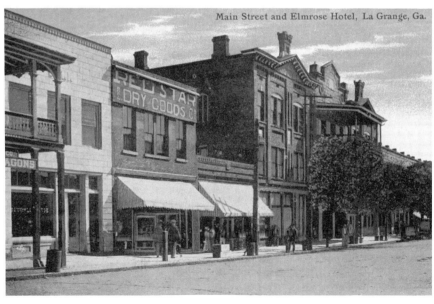

Main Street and Elmrose Hotel, La Grange, Ga.

Depot St. looking north, Abbeville, Ga. 5434

Pub by Art Novelty Pub Co.

Adel in 1910.

Paulk's Drug Store and Bank of Alapaha, ALAPAHA, GA

18

South Side of Broad St. Albany, Ga.

LAMAR STREET.   AMERICUS, GA.

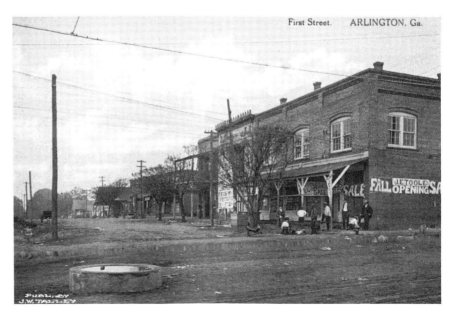

First Street.   ARLINGTON, Ga.

19

Broad Street, Athens, Ga.

Peachtree & Marietta Streets, Atlanta, Ga.

Mitchell St. looking West from Whitehall St., Atlanta, Ga.

Copyright 1905 by the Rotograph Co.

G 13636 Busy Morning on Broad Street, Augusta, Ga.

BAINBRIDGE, GA.   Broad St., looking South.

CONFEDERATE FLAG POLE, ERECTED 1861, BLAKELY, GA.
ONLY FLAG POLE STANDING IN SOUTH.
S. A. WALDROP, PUBL.   Hand-Colored.

Main Street, looking North,
Boston, Ga.

South Side Main St.,
Canton, Ga.

Main Street, looking East.
CARTERSVILLE, Ga.

22

Main Street, looking East, Coleman, Ga.

Night Scene on Broad St. looking North from 10th St. Columbus Ga.

Street Scene, Covington, Ga.

Handcolored.

Business Section on Main St., Looking West, showing Confederate Monument, Crawfordville, Ga.

MAIN STREET, CUMBERLAND, GA.

West Side of Square, Cuthbert, Ga.

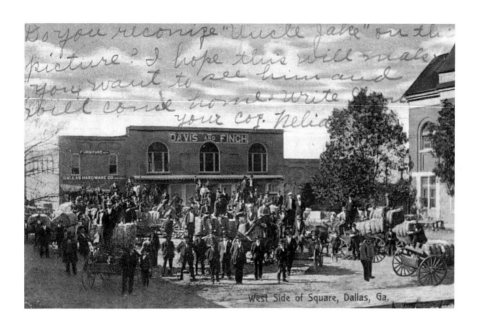

Do you reconige "Uncle Jake" on the picture? I hope this will make you want to see him and he'll come home write to us your cos. Nelia

West Side of Square, Dallas, Ga.

DAWSON, GA.   Main St., looking North

A Mountain Scene at Dillard, Ga.

Eatonton, Ga.

ON THE SQUARE, ELBERTON, GA.

B2135D5   Cor. Oglethorpe and Broad Sts., Ellaville, Ga.

Grant Street, Fitzgerald, Ga.

East Johnson St., Forsyth, Ga.

BUSINESS PORTION OF MAIN STREET, FORT VALLEY, GA.

PUB. BY DR. J. B. GEORGE, DRUGGIST.   GAINESVILLE, GA., ON A BUSY DAY.

GRIFFIN, GA. N, Hill St.

Looking Down Lawson Street, Hahira, Ga.

Pub. by Hahira Drug Co.

29

Jackson Street, Hawkinsville, Ga.

THE COLEMAN CORNER,
HELENA, GA.

North Side Public Square,
Jefferson, Ga.

30

View looking toward the Square, Jesup, Ga

Perry Street, Lawrenceville, Ga.

Main Street, Locust Grove, Ga.

31

WINDSOR PARK AND COURT HOUSE, McRAE, GA.

View on Wayne Street, Milledgeville, Ga.

Cotton Ave., Millen, Ga.

OAK ST. LOOKING SOUTH, MILLTOWN, GA.

WEST SIDE OF SQUARE, MONTICELLO, GA.

West Broad Street, Moultrie, Ga.

33

Cotton Scene on Public Square, Newnan, Ga.

SCENE CN ELM ST. LOOKING NORTH. ODESSADALE, GA.

Lee Street from South, Quitman, Ga.

Broad Street. ROME, Ga. Showing First Monument erected to Daughters of Confederacy.

CHICKAMAUGA AVE ROSSVILL GA.

Bull Street looking N. Savannah, Ga.

Broughton Street, Savannah, Ga.

Broughton Street, looking East, by Night, Savannah, Ga.

Business Street, Sylvester, Georgia.

Street Scene, Talbotton, Ga.

A 13500 Broad Street, Thomasville, Ga.

Am going to write you soon.
Maude

MARKET SQUARE.   WASHINGTON, GA.

37

Main Street, Washington, Ga.

Broad Street, looking South, Winder, Ga.

ZEBULON, GA.   Street Scene

A 13587 The Flatiron Bldg., Atlanta, Ga.

"The Great White Way," Atlanta, Ga.

Whitehall Street,
Business Center of Atlanta. Ga.
The Great White Way.

PUBLIC BUILDINGS

"Travelers say that we have the most and highest buildings of any city except New York City."

Then as now, Georgia's domed Capitol in Atlanta was the state's seat of government—the place where laws were passed, political battles won or lost, and public careers made or broken. Government at the town and county level resided in the city halls and courthouses. The architects who designed these buildings knew exactly what they were doing: the columns, the domes, the details borrowed from the Greeks, even the clock, told the people that here was the law, the civil authority, the court's authority to sit in judgment and dispense justice.

Interior of the Auditorium Atlanta Ga.

HABERSHAM COUNTY'S COURT HOUSE, ERECTED 1832, TORN DOWN 1898, CLARKSVILLE, GA.

Here disputes were settled, votes were counted, and taxes levied.

These are the public buildings that were so popular with the photographers who took the views we see on early post cards and with the collectors who bought them. They encapsulated the town, set it off from towns that had nothing more than a block of stores or a water tank to identify them. Occasionally one of the cards, like the view of the Jasper County courthouse in Monticello, does more than document a building. In this case the camera has recorded a 1902 election. Five years later the building was demolished. Many of these buildings are in fact no longer standing. The old Coweta County courthouse in Newnan was torn down in 1904, the Toombs County courthouse burned in 1917, the Stewart County courthouse in 1923. The historic value of such views is obvious.

NEW JAIL BUILDING
FITZERALD, GA.

No. 1 Engine House,
Marietta Fire Dept., Marietta, Ga.

50·18

Wilcox County Jail, Abbeville, Ga. 2481

Pub. by Art Novelty Pub. Co.

A 13650 City Hall & Stand Pipe, Lamar Street, Americus, Ga.

13510 City Hall, Athens, Ga.

4949 GRADY HOSPITAL. ATLANTA, GA.

Georgia State Capitol, Atlanta, Ga.

STATE OF GEORGIA 1799

Hon. Hoke Smith, Gov.

State of Georgia.

Children's Hospital, Augusta, Ga.

CITY HALL AND FIRE DEPT.
BAINBRIDGE. GA.

PIERCE COUNTY COURT HOUSE, BLACKSHEAR, GA.

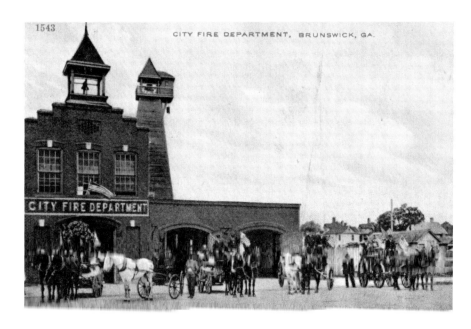

1543

CITY FIRE DEPARTMENT, BRUNSWICK, GA.

CITY FIRE DEPARTMENT

Court House,
Buena Vista, Ga.

Grady
County
Prison,
Cairo, Ga.

Pub. by Grady
Pharmacy.

Court House,
Columbus, Ga.

No. 3—Hardman Sanatorium, Commerce, Ga.   N. C. ALEXANDER, PUB.

Pumping Station, Cordele, Ga.

B1019A5   Court House, Dahlonega, Ga.

P. 6. Friday there was 44 new boy to 38 old
Every one seems anxious to begin.
Rufe Ed has been down in bed
a week now but is
better. The doctors
dont know what it is,
they say he had symptom
of Typhoid.

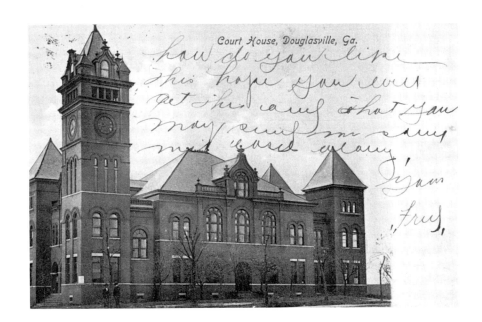

Court House, Douglasville, Ga.

how do you like this hope you will get this and what you may send me any and over many your Frances

City Hall and Fire Department, Dublin, Ga.

CITY HALL
CITY HALL

Courthouse, Eatonton, Ga.

Court House, Fairburn, Ga.

B480E6

Griffin Hospital, Griffin, Ga.

County Court House, Hartwell, Ga,   Photo by Hall, Feb. 10, 1908.

48

Court House Building, Jasper, Ga.

Stewart County Court House, Lumpkin, Ga.

Pub. by The New Drug Store

Toombs County Court House, Lyons, Ga.

Macon Hospital, Macon, Ga.

Court House, Confederate Monument and
Opera House, Macon, Ga.

Fire Department, Macon, Ga.

Jasper County Court House.   Built 1838.   Monticello, Ga.   Primary Election, 1902.

The Old Court House, Newnan, Ga.

L. E. ROUGHTON.
COURT HOUSE, PERRY, GA., HOUSTON. CO.

Courthouse, Sandersville, Ga.

SAVANNAH, GA.   Telfair Hospital, for Females.

4816

The City Hall (with Jail below),
"Wasaw City"
Thunderbolt, Savannah, Ga.

PUBLIC LIBRARY SAVANNAH GA.

COURT HOUSE, SUMMERVILLE, GA.

From L. B. McGinnis
Summerville Ga.

FRANK · P · MILBURN · & · CO ·
ARCHITECTS · WASHINGTON · D·C

THOMASTON, GA.
Upson County New Court House

53

Dooly County Court House, Vienna, Ga.
B2678A1

COURT HOUSE, WARRENTON, GA.

Old Court House,
Torn Down 1902,
Washington, Ga.

54

Many thanks for your thoughtfulness. The views are pretty. Jno P Barney[?]

GREETINGS FROM PICTURESQUE AMERICA

Hon. A. J. CROVATT, Mayor.

CITY HALL, BRUNSWICK, GA.

Arthur Livingston, Publisher, New York. 740

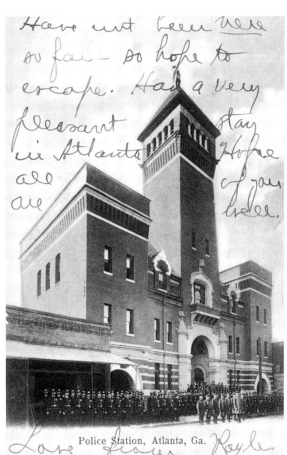

Have not been here so far — so hope to escape. Had a very pleasant stay in Atlanta. Hope all of you are well.

Love from Royle[?]

Police Station, Atlanta, Ga.

Sep., 19, 1907

ALAYON-GREEN DRUG CO.

MARY WILLIS LIBRARY, WASHINGTON, GA.

I received your card. Hope you will keep your promise. Write

55

RESIDENCES

"There are a great many 2 story homes here. Very pretty."

Many of the private residences that were preserved on picture post cards were predictably large and leave the impression that all Georgians lived in two-story homes with white columns. Even before *Gone with the Wind* and Tara, the South had a fondness for white columns. The houses were of course singled out for the same reason one would point them out to visitors on a drive through the town: a matter of community pride. They represented affluence. Or they were old enough to be called, even in 1908 or 1910 and less than fifty years removed from the war, "antebellum." Next door and around the corner were more modest homes, usually of frame construction, usually one-story with an open gallery, like the

Augusta, Ga.

residence of H. J. Peavy in Byron. And on the back streets and in the black neighborhoods, the houses were even smaller and more modest, frequently one room behind another.

One Georgia residence we will unfortunately never see is the one mentioned in this brief note from a 1914 card: "I miss you and mama so much. The hen nest on top of your house has six eggs in it." The houses on the post cards were usually the homes of the town's leading citizens, and their size is less a reflection of the size of early twentieth century families than it is a comment on the importance of status. Bankers and judges and railroad presidents were expected to occupy large houses. These were the homes that by the middle years of the century had become "white elephants"—their owners had died or moved to the suburbs and they were fated to be cut up into multifamily apartments or converted to YMCAs or funeral parlors.

Eatonton, Ga.

Residence S. B. Brown, Albany, Ga.

Residence of J. S. Cowart.   ARLINGTON, Ga.

PHOL. BY
J.W.TALLEY

VIEW ON PRINCE AVENUE, ATHENS, GA.

58

Residence of
Judge Hamilton McWhorter
Athens, Georgia

Dr. William A. Carlton Residence,
750 South Milledge Avenue, Athens,
Ga.

Atlanta, Ga.

59

ATLANTA, GA
Governor's
Mansion.

ATLANTA, GA.

Augusta, Ga.

Jones Residence, Boston, Ga.

Bona Allen Residence, Buford, Ga.

Residence of H. J. Peavy, Byron, Ga.

HOME OF SAM JONES,
CARTERSVILLE, GA

Old Southern Residence, COLUMBUS, Ga.

RESIDENCE OF C. J. HOOD,
COMMERCE, GA.

63

Residence of A. Whitaker, Velta, Ga., near Conyers.

The Carnegie Mansion, Dungeness, Cumberland Island, Ga.

Residence of E. L. Bacon, Doerun, Ga.

Bellevue Avenue, Dublin, Ga.

RESIDENCE W. O. JONES, ELBERTON, GA.

FORT GAINES, GA,
Ante-Bellum Home

One of Grantville's
Pretty Residences.

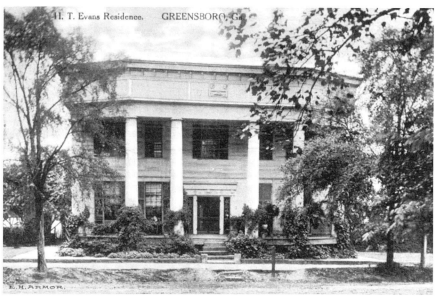

I. T. Evans Residence.   GREENSBORO, Ga.

E. H. ARMOR.

Residence of E. W. Copelon.   GREENSBORO, Ga.

Fine Residence. Griffin, Ga.

Benjamin H. Hill Home.
LA GRANGE, Ga.

BRADFIELD DRUG CO.

Lindale Ga. A group of residences.
Brittain Bro. Dept. Store.

67

A Colonial Home, Macon, Ga., Residence of A. Block.

Governor Brown's Residence, Whitlock Avenue, Marietta, Ga.

1850 Grey Gables, Misses Crocketts, 500 Cherokee St., Marietta, Ga.

Residence of W. T. Brightwell, Maxeys, Ga.

Dr. W. D. Kennedy's Residence. Metter, Ga.

Residence View on Greenville Street, Newnan, Ga.

RESIDENCE OF S. A. PATTERSON, ROUND OAK, GEORGIA

Vinnign House, Rutledge, Ga.

Residence of Mr. D. P. Hale, Sandersville; Ga.

Savannah, Ga.

Residence of Mrs. C. F. Sasser, Senoia, Ga.

Residence of S. G. Williams, Swainsboro, Ga.

Darling's Southern Home - Tallapoosa Georgia

Residence of Mayor H. M. Franklin, Tennille, Ga.

Greenwood Plantation, near House.   THOMASVILLE, Ga.

Toccoa, Ga.

SCHOOLS AND COLLEGES

*"I have spent many days in this house
and got some few whippings in it."*

In Georgia the battle over public education had already been fought by the turn of the century, but there were still important questions to be settled. Foremost of these was whether the segregated school system then in place would continue—a question not resolved until the 1950s, and then only by federal court order. In the early 1900s white children went to school in white schools and black children in black schools, the great majority of both at the elementary level. In rural areas many of the schools held their classes in churches or in one-room schoolhouses with potbellied stoves for heat in winter and open windows for ventilation when the weather turned warmer.

Peace Hall, the Girl's Dormitory of the Albany Bible and Manual Training Institute, and the Principal, Dr. Holley, Albany, Ga.

Public School, Rutledge, Ga.

But there was a will to learn and a cadre of dedicated teachers, black and white, and though progress was slow it was certain.

The early post card views reflect a time when the new high school was a source of community pride in the larger towns and cities. Beyond the elementary schools and public high schools there were the colleges, state- or church-supported as well as private. Many of these were photographed for the companies that published post card views, and as a consequence the cards are a valuable documentary record, in some cases the only evidence left of how these schools looked. Interior views like that of the sitting room at the Martha Berry School for Girls are especially useful. As might be expected, a great many of the views show buildings or scenes on the University of Georgia campus. But many of the smaller schools, including some no longer in existence, are also represented.

High School, Waycross, Ga.

Public School Building, West Point, Ga.

DORMITORY OF THE G.N.C AND B.I. ABBEVILLE, GA.

AMERICUS INSTITUTE, Americus, Ga.

BOYS' DORMITORY

DINING HALL

MAIN BUILDING

GIRLS' DORMITORY

GIRLS' DORMITORY

A 13621 State Normal School, Athens, Ga.

Buildings on the Campus, Athens, Ga.

Send your Boy to the State College of Agriculture, University of Georgia
Athens, Georgia

Tuition free. You may enter now. Cost for nine months about $150.00

Avail yourself of the free services of the Extension or Information Dept.

COURSES OFFERED:—Four-Year leading to B. S. A. degree
One-Year or Practical Farmers' Course—No. entrance examinations. Three-Months' Course, Jan. 2 to April 2, 1911; Cost of board, etc. about $50   Cotton Graders' Course, Jan. 2 to Feb. 2, 1911, Cost of board, etc. about $25   Farmers' Course or Cotton School, Jan 2 to 13, 1911, Cost of board, etc. about $15 to $25.
Write for Information to ANDREW M. SOULE, President.

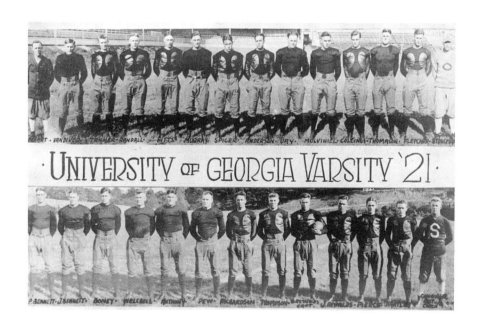

A 13622 Lucy Cobb Institute, Athens, Ga.

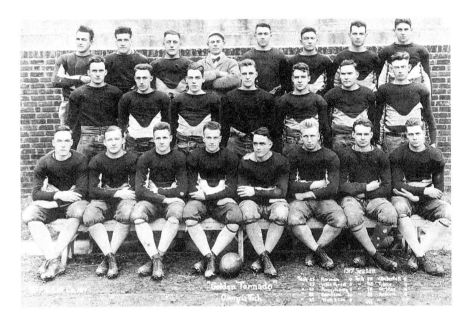

Main Building, Georgia School of Technology, Atlanta, Ga.

CLOSING EXERCISES
1904

Sermon before the Societies
Rev. P. J. Bryant, D. D.
May 1, 3 p. m.

Commencement Sermon
Rev. E. R. Carter, D. D.
May 15, 3 p. m.

Class Day Exercises
May 16, 2.30 p. m.

Alumnæ Meeting
May 17, 7.30 p. m.

Commencement
May 18, 10 a. m.

You are cordially invited
to attend

SPELLMAN SEMINARY.

Atlanta, Ga.,

Millie M. Takley.

Cox Female College, College Park, Atlanta, Ga.

Dear Leta: How do you like school. I hope
you aren't very homesick. Devotedly Fannie

Richmond Academy. Augusta, Ga.

F. E. Williams, Augusta, Ga.

Arthur Livingston, Publisher, New York. 748

RISLEY GRAMMAR SCHOOL, (COLORED)
BRUNSWICK, GA.

I B GRADE   BUFORD PUBLIC SCHOOL

The Model School, Cass Station, Ga.

CASS STATION, GA.

Public School.   CEDARTOWN, Ga.

THE LIBRARY. SYLVAN TERRACE SCHOOL.

COLUMBUS, GA.   Girard Branch, Eagle & Phoenix Free Kindergarten

SCHOOL HOUSE, CUMMINGS, GA.

Andrew Female College, Cuthbert, Ga.

N. G. A. College, Dahlonega, Ga.

B1019D5

82

High School, Danielsville, Georgia

Agnes Scott College, Decatur, Ga.
Six miles from Atlanta, an Institution ranking among the very Best
Female Colleges in the South.

Eton, Ga.

Fitzgerald's First School House. In "Shacktown Days," 1895.

Thought that this would interest a school maam Pat.

Sold by Adams Candy Ktchien.   Souvenir of Fitzgerald Ga.

South Car School House, Fitzgerald, Ga.

BOYS OF FREDERICA SCHOOL.

On the Athletic Field, Brenau College, Gainsville, Ga.

High School and City Water Tank, Lawrenceville, Ga.

Ludowici, Ga.

A 13574   Wesleyan Female College, Macon, Ga.

MACON, GA.   Mercer University and Chapel.

Foot Ball Eleven, 1907.   Georgia Military College, Milledgeville, Ga.

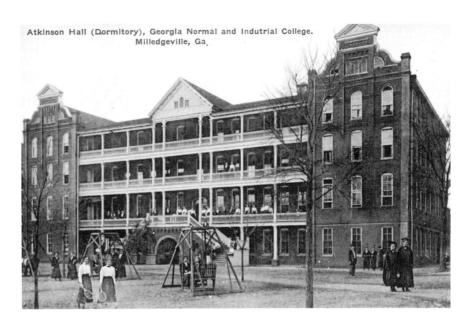
Atkinson Hall (Dormitory), Georgia Normal and Indutrial College.
Milledgeville, Ga.

Georgia Military College.
Milledgeville, Ga.

There are 500 boys here.

R.H.WOOTTEN.

SITTING ROOM,
MARTHA BERRY SCHOOL
FOR GIRLS
MOUNT BERRY, GA.

Boys' Dormitory---Union Baptist Institute, Mt. Vernon, Ga.

School of Telegraphy and Business College, Newnan, Ga.

THE BRYAN NORMAL INSTITUTE AND COLLEGE STREET, PEMBROKE, GA.

Public School, Rome, Ga.

Colored Public School, Rome, Ga.

Temple Graded School, Temple, Ga.

89

Allen Normal and Industrial School.   THOMASVILLE, Ga.

Toccoa Falls Institute, Toccoa Falls, Ga.

08008 Washington, Ga.
St. Joseph's Academy.

Baseball Players, Piedmont College,
Demorest, Ga.

Public School Bldg., Fairburn, Ga.

CHURCHES

"This is where I got 'religion.'"

From Georgia's beginnings as a colony, religion was an important part of the life of the people. Churches and synagogues met their spiritual needs and at the same time served a social purpose, as places that brought them into contact with their neighbors. Church socials and church picnics were among the most popular forms of recreation. The churches also served as a stabilizing force at a time when there was a movement from "the country" to the towns and cities. In Atlanta alone there were 121 churches in 1900. Every town had a Baptist church, and most had a Methodist church as well. In

Jerusalem Lutheran Church
Ebenezer, Georgia

many communities there were also Presbyterian, Episcopal, Roman Catholic, and Lutheran congregations. As late as the early decades of the twentieth century there was a strong sense of identification with a denomination that had not yet blurred the distinction between a Catholic and a Protestant or a Baptist and a Methodist. What the picture post cards show us is a small-town Georgia that was predominantly Protestant.

The appearance of these churches on the post cards reflects the pride that people took in them—a pride seen in some of the messages inscribed by the senders. The cards also show us a time when there were dinners on the grounds and revivals and camp meetings, and when the churches erected parsonages to house their ministers. At least one of these small-town churches—the Baptist church in Plains—would later become famous, but that was something no one could have foreseen in the early 1900s.

Baptist Church, Indian Spring, Ga.

3593   Christ Church, Savannah, Ga.

Colored baptizing in Flint River Albany, Ga.

OUTDOOR TABERNACLE
ASHBURN, GEORGIA

ATHENS, Ga. Presbyterian Church.

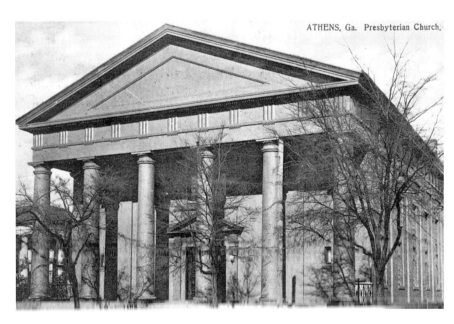

New Broughton Tabernacle,
Atlanta, Ga.

St. James' M. E. Church and Cenotaph, Augusta, Ga.

206,518. (V)

Austell, Ga.

This is a new parsonage that has been built since you left here. It is just below the church. Willie.

Episcopal Church and Broughton St., Bainbridge, Ga.

First Baptist Church,
Barwick, Ga.

Methodist Church, Butler, Ga.

Sam Jones's Tabernacle, Cartersville, Ga.

CHESTER, GA.
METHODIST CHURCH.   CHESTER HIGH SCHOOL.   BAPTIST CHURCH.

Methodist Church, Cuthbert, Ga.

Colored Baptist Church, Darien, Ga.

Union Cong'l. Church Demorest Ga

Dedicated Nov. 29-1905.

M. E. Church, Forsyth, Ga.

FIRST BAPTIST CHURCH, GAINESVILLE, GA.

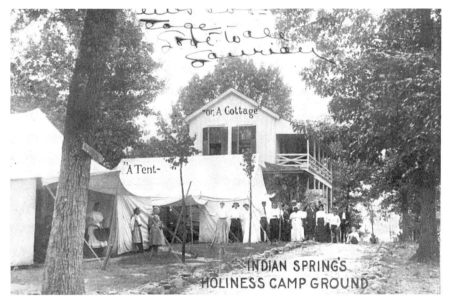

"or, A Cottage"

"A Tent-"

INDIAN SPRINGS
HOLINESS CAMP GROUND

M.E. CHURCH AND COURT HOUSE, JESUP, GA.

99

REV. J. B. PHILLIPS,
OF MACON, GA.,

WILL LEAD IN AN EVANGEL-
ISTIC CAMPAIGN AT THE

NORTH BAPTIST CHURCH
234 WEST 11TH STREET

MEETINGS EVERY NIGHT EXCEPT
SATURDAY, FROM OCT. 4 TO 18,

A LARGE AUXILIARY CHOIR WILL ASSIST
IN SINGING NEW SONGS OF THE GOSPEL

CHRISTIAN WORKERS ARE INVITED TO BRING FRIENDS

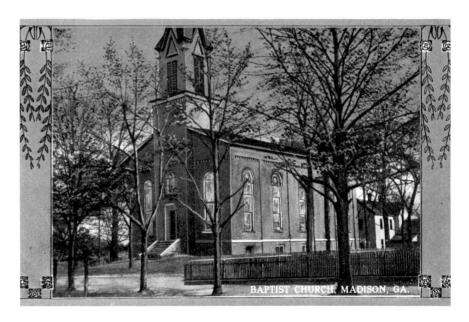

BAPTIST CHURCH, MADISON, GA.

First Methodist Church, Millen, Ga.

A. M. E. Church, Quitman, Ga.

Christ Church Frederica,
St. Simons Island, Ga.

Greek Orthodox Church,
Savannah, Ga.

Cathedral of St. John the Baptist, Savannah, Ga.

Baptist Church, Senoia, Ga.

Baptist Church, Tallapoosa, Ga.

METHODIST CHURCH, TRION, GA.

A 13535 Grace Church, Waycross, Ga.

Methodist Parsonage, Center St., Winder, Ga

103

Christian Science Church, Atlanta, Ga.

Baptist Church, Bowdon, Ga.

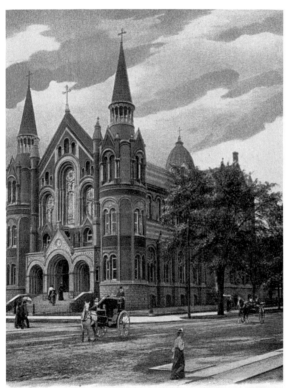

AUGUSTA, GA. Sacred Heart Church.

Primitive Baptist Church, Graymont, Ga.

The Presbyterian Church, Dawson, Ga.

Episcopal Church, Greensboro, Ga.

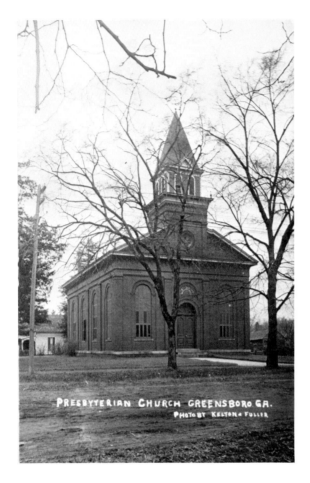

PRESBYTERIAN CHURCH GREENSBORO GA.
PHOTO BY KELTON & FULLER

BAPTIST CHURCH PLAINS GA.

It is also good looking inside.

MACON, GA. St. Joseph's Catholic Church.

Methodist Church, Watkinsville, Ga.

M. E. CHURCH SUWANEE.

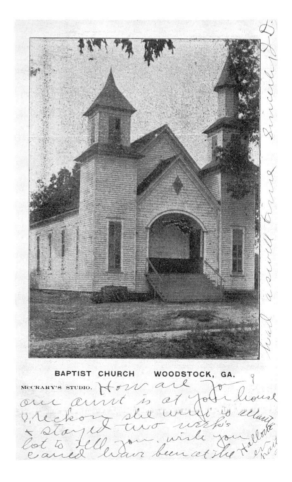

BAPTIST CHURCH   WOODSTOCK, GA.

McCRARY'S STUDIO.

AGRICULTURE

"If we had more currency and less cotton, things would be much better in these parts."

Georgia, like other southern states, was predominantly rural and agricultural in the early decades of the century, and cotton was preeminently the crop of the region. The state's economy was to a large extent dependent upon the success of the year's crop, and fortunes could, and frequently did, rest on such variables as rain or the lack of it, and after 1913 on the boll weevil. The post card views of cotton fields, gins, and compresses, and of town squares and city streets jammed with wagons loaded with bales, leave no doubt as to the importance of cotton. Small towns sometimes measured themselves against other small towns by how many gins they had. Farmers

Cotton Scene.
Calhoun, Ga.

ELBERTA PEACHES
Dalton, Ga.

competed with one another for the distinction of bringing in the year's first bale. One of the cards in this collection records for us the date on which W. A. Brannon delivered two hundred bales of cotton to Newnan.

There were other crops that were a part of the Georgia economy—peaches, for instance, especially the Elberta peach, famous long before anyone had heard of the Vidalia onion. Corn was one of the major crops in the early 1900s, as was tobacco. Many of the state's farmers grew sugar cane. Others raised livestock or poultry (the card of the rooster and hen pulling the wagonload of eggs is of course a trick of the photographer), and dairying accounted for a sizable amount of income from agriculture. Eighty-five percent of the state's population lived on farms or outside towns and cities in 1900. But the movement from the farms to the small towns and from the small towns to the cities had already begun, and Georgia would become slowly but increasingly more industrial.

Kennesaw, Ga.

Pelham, Ga.

Depot during Elberta Rush, Adairsville, Ga.

Iron Mountain Shed, Elberta Rush, Adairsville, Ga.

Cotton Ginnery, Augusta, Ga.

SUGAR CANE FIELD ON WIGHT'S INGLESIDE PLANTATION, NEAR CAIRO, GA.
PUB. BY WIGHT & BROWNE, CAIRO, GA.

OLD FASHION CANE GRINDING, NEAR CAIRO, GA.
PUB. BY WIGHT & BROWNE, CAIRO, GA.

AN AVENUE OF PECANS, PECAN GROVE FARM, CAIRO, GA.

PUB. BY WIGHT & BROWNE, CAIRO, GA.

MR. T. H. GIGNILLIOT'S RICE PLANTATION.
NEAR DARIEN, GA.

Cotton-field near Eatonton, Ga.

Old Corn and Cotton Palace, Fitzgerald, Ga.

COTTON GIN.   FITZGERALD, GA.

Cotton Ware House, Fort Valley, Ga.

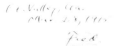

Buffalo Cotton Yard, Madison, Ga.

Weighing Cotton in the Field,
near Madison, Ga.

114

Vegetable Garden, near Nahunta, Ga.

Saving Excel Watermelon Seed, Andersonville, Ga. for O.K. Jelks & Son, Quitman, Ga.   (Note Junior Member of firm next to wagon)   18700

B8138   Hog Raising, Brooks Co., Quitman, Ga.

Broad Street, Cotton Scene.   ROME, Ga.

P. J. OSTERMAN FARM
St. George, Ga. 1910

FERN CREST DAIRY, Sandersville, Ga.

Terrapin Farm,
Isle of Hope, Savannah, Ga.

Cotten Gin.
An Old Timer
Near Tallapoosa, Ga.

Tifton Cotton Compress, Tifton, Ga.
Will handle about 30,000 bales for the Season of 1913-14.

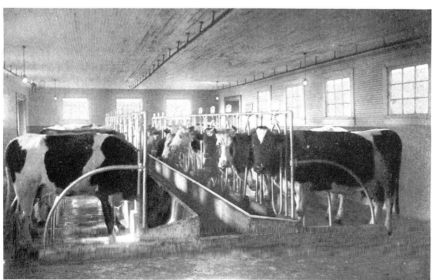

FEEDING TIME, TRION DAIRY, THE TRION COMPANY, TRION, GA.

Yours truly,
North Georgia Warehouse Co.
DENNIS BARRETT, Prop'r.

Cotton Exchange, Savannah, Ga.

A Record Breaking Load of Cotton, Savannah, Ga.

Commerce and Industry

*"Business very good.
Have to stay over another day,
got 40 orders so far."*

Well into the second decade of the century, Georgia was overwhelmingly rural and overwhelmingly agricultural, but the efforts of men like Henry Grady had begun to shape the outline of a South that was moving toward industrialization. By the early 1900s the mills had indeed come to the cotton, and textile mills were not the only factories that dotted the landscape. Dalton had its flour mills, and Darien its canning factories. Power companies were lighting more and more homes across the state, though rural electrification was still in the future. The lumber and turpentine industries were booming, the

COLUMBUS, GA   Georgia Home Building

Cotton Mill, Hawkinsville, Ga.

ports of Savannah and Brunswick busy with commerce, and enterprise and advertising had carried Coca-Cola's name well beyond Georgia.

New buildings were going up in the business sections of the larger towns, and one post card sender bragged that Waycross, otherwise quiet ("No liquors sold, no moving picture shows"), had "about 25 drug stores." The department store was replacing the general store, even in some of the smaller towns. Much of the state's economic growth was attributable to the automobile, which brought with it related businesses such as dealerships, garages, and service stations in addition to automobile manufactories. Atlanta would emerge as a major distribution point for auto sales and a center for the "Good Roads" movement. But other cities also felt the surge of business activity that characterized the period.

Interior, Vason Brothers Drug Store, Madison, Ga.

C780   H. S. Burch, Jeweler, Royston, Ga.

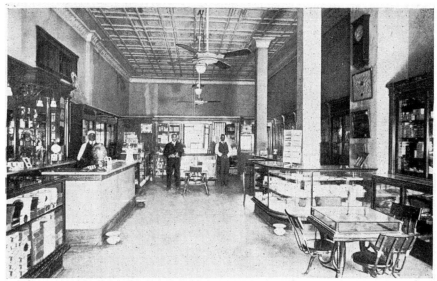

THE E. D. HARRIS DRUG STORE, ATHENS, GA.

The Housing of one of Athens' (Ga.)
Representative Businesses,
Michael Bros. Co.

ATLANTA'S BUSIEST CORNER.

MILTON W. ARROWOOD CO.
EDISON PHONOGRAPH DISTRIBUTORS
ATLANTA, GEORGIA
TERMS—Free Trial. Half Cash. Balance $1.00 a Month

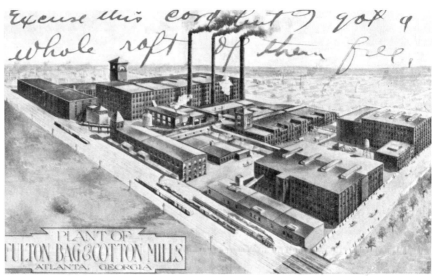

PLANT OF
FULTON BAG & COTTON MILLS
ATLANTA, GEORGIA
BRANCHES
NEW YORK, N.Y.   ST. LOUIS, MO.   NEW ORLEANS, LA.   DALLAS, TEX.

Sibley Mills, Augusta, Ga.

Manufacturing Concrete Blocks and Pipes, Bethlehem, Ga.

F. S. Nash Delivering Water at Brunswick, Ga.

Mallory Steam Ship Docks, Brunswick, Ga.

Cartersville, Ga.?

B425C5   Merchants and Farmers Bank Building, Claxton, Ga.

A 13546   "Lunch Time at the Factory", Columbus, Ga.

R. F. Strickland Co., Department Store, CONCORD, Ga.

Webster—Mann Co. Department Store, Clothing Department, Cordele, Ga.

Dalton Flour Mills, Dalton, Ga.

BOOM AND SAW MILL, DARIEN, GA.

127

CANNING FACTORY, BUTLER'S ISLAND, DARIEN, GA.

DOUGLASVILLE BANKING COMPANY, DOUGLASVILLE, GA.

J. L. SELMAN & SON, PUBLISHERS   26.28

Store of C. D. Dudley & Son, General Merchants, Dublin, Ga.

Red Cross Pharmacy   RED CROSS PHARMACY, EASTMAN, GA.

Photography Studio, 117 South Lee Street, Fitzgerald, Ga.

LAKE WARNER, GAINESVILLE, GA.

BEAVER CREEK MILLS NEAR GREENSBORO GA.
PHOTO BY KELTON & FULLER

McCommons-Thompson-Boswell Co.,
Largest Department Store in Middle Georgia.
GREENSBORO, Ga.

E. H. ARMOR.

One of the
Busy Places
in Griffin,
Ga.,
McClure's

Byrd-Matthews Lumber Co.   Helen, Georgia.   (Capacity, 125,000 feet per day.)

Power House,
Central Georgia Power Co.,
Jackson, Ga.

Jester's Old Mill, Jonesboro, Ga., near Atlanta.

Financial Acorns.

Great oaks of financial success grow from very small acorns. A small sum opens an account in our bank; but to have a big, healthy financial tree, you should be persistent in your depositing.

Systematic depositing is the root of financial independence. Get deeply rooted in the habit of banking; then you will branch out into better things, and be safe against any ill wind that blows.

Dollars are financial acorns. Plant them in our bank and watch them grow.

Bank of Kingston

Kingston, Georgia

Your Deposits Absolutely Insured Against Loss

You may send us your large or small deposits by mail. Interest Paid on Time Deposits

386. THE RED STAR SHOE STORE, LA GRANGE, GA.
"STAR BRAND SHOES ARE BETTER."

Schaub, Photo.

La Grange's Oldest Grocery House, J. C. Roper. La Grange, Ga.

Photo by Schaub.

Pub. by Adolph Selige for The Reporter Pub. Co. La Grange, Ga.

Lake Burton and Dam as seen from an Aeroplane

THIS beautiful body of water forms the largest reservoir of the Georgia Railway & Power Company. The dam is 116 feet high and forms a lake covering 2,775 acres, with a shore line of 64 miles. The lake is famous as one of the greatest fishing resorts in the South.

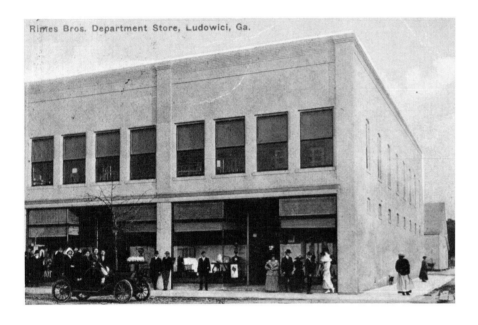

Rimes Bros. Department Store, Ludowici, Ga.

FIRST FLOOR

OUR NEW HOME
HEADQUARTERS EVERYTHING MUSICAL

THE F. A. GUTTENBERGER CO.
CUSTIS N. GUTTENBERGER
MANAGER

Triangular Block   MACON, GA.

FRONT
Weber Pianos
Kranich & Bach
McPhail Pianos
Smith & Barnes
Bailey Pianos

REAR
Seybold Reed Pipe Organs
Violins, Mandolins, Guitars, Banjos
Victor and Columbia
Talking Machines
Sheet Music, Half Price

Cochran's Mill, Meldrim, Ga.

ONLY the BEST PAYS

WE ARE PLANTING HONEST METHODS AND GROWING PUBLIC CONFIDENCE WE ARE HERE TO STAY

1911   May   1911

S.	M.	T.	W.	T.	F.	S.
	1	2	3	4	5	6
7	8	9	10	11	12	13
14	15	16	17	18	19	20
21	22	23	24	25	26	27
28	29	30	31			

Our business is GROWING, thank you! We planted the right kind of seeds when we began business. We began by selling only RELIABLE merchandise, and we've never been able to persuade ourselves that it would pay us to sell any other kind.

Why not buy YOUR hardware from US?

Exclusive Agents
Superb and Charter Oak Ranges
American Field and Garden Fence
Diamond Edge Tools, Oliver Chilled Plows

MONTICELLO HARDWARE COMPANY,
Monticello, Ga.

R. D. Cole Co., Showing Offices and part of Force, Newnan, Ga.

RABUN COUNTY GA

INTERIOR
SHROPSHIRE
BOOK STORE
307 BROAD ST.
ROME, GA.

Wyatt Jewelry Co.
304 BROAD STREET, ROME, GA.

Postmarked September 23, 1908, Rossville, Ga.

Home of "Savannah Poster Adv Service"
Price & Mapes Owners Savannah Ga

Artesian Water Mill, Tarboro, Ga.

Interior of
Wilson & Terry's Drug Store Thomasville Ga.

Cherokee Saw Mill Co., Thomasville, Ga.

Idle Hour Cafe, Thomson, Ga.

Hebard Cypress Mills, Waycross, Ga.

Flanigan & Flanigan, Pianos, Buggies and Automobiles, Winder, Ga.

White's Mill.
Winder, Ga.

Dipping Gum from the Pine for Rosin and Turpentine in South Georgia on A. B. and A. R. R.

Chipping the Pine Tree for the Flow of Gum. South Georgia on A. B. and A. R. R.

Goat Rock Dam and Power Station, near Columbus, Ga.   Height of Dam, 70 feet;
length, 1,500 feet.   Area of Pond, 1,000 acres.   Ultimate capacity, 40,000 H. P.
Transmission Lines to West Point, LaGrange and Newman.

Advertising Card for Goat Rock Dam
and Power Station, near Columbus, Ga.

HYDRAULIC MINING, CHESTATEE MINES

Mining Gold with a "Water Giant,"
Lumpkin County, Ga.

BANKING HOUSE
OF
THE TATTNALL BANK
REIDSVILLE, GA.
CAPITAL, SURPLUS AND PROFITS $75,000.00
ORGANIZED IN 1900

W. J. Waters & Son, Jewelry Store, Sylvania, Ga.

TRANSPORTATION

"I wish I could see you but I can't until the roads get better."

At about the time when many of the views in this book were being published, Orville and Wilbur Wright soared into the air for a few seconds over a sand spit in North Carolina. But in 1903 the age of aviation was yet a while away, and the age of the automobile was just beginning. One sender bragged on one of these cards that "about twenty autos a week make the trip from Savannah to Atlanta." The messages on the cards make it clear that automobile travel was fraught with uncertainties. "Had a flat tire & had to change that & a down pour of rain hindered me," wrote another sender.

Street Car, Athens, Ga.

Georgians still traveled by rail. The passenger train was the preferred mode of long-distance, and even short-distance, travel. The railroad terminal or depot was a common subject in the picture post card views, and incidentally the place where many cards were sold and mailed. Indeed it was the railroad that bound the state together, and that made Atlanta the southern metropolis that it became. The railroads would continue to dominate transportation into and beyond the 1920s. But the automobile brought with it a sense of independence and a spirit of adventure. Drivers participated in road tours and endurance races. Some of the early automobile races, most notably the International Grand Prize Race of the Automobile Club of America and the Vanderbilt Cup Race, were held in Savannah. New automobiles meant better roads, sturdier bridges, paved highways, and automobile dealerships where one could buy a roadster or a touring car for a few hundred dollars. Automobiles and buggies and wagons shared the same street in these post card views from the early 1900s, but the horses' days were numbered.

STR. "HESSIE" THAT PLIES BETWEEN BRUNSWICK AND DARIEN, GA.

PAXSON'S LAUNCH AT BOHANNON'S FERRY, ABBEVILLE, GA.

Steam Boat on Flint River, Albany, Ga.

AMERICUS, GA.

October 22. 1906.   Yours Sincerely   G.H.E.

SEABOARD PASSENGER STATION.   ATHENS, GA.

Atlanta Terminal
Station,
Atlanta, Ga.

Union Station, Atlanta, Ga.

Western & Atlantic R. R. Bridge over the Chattahoochee River, near ATLANTA, Ga.

Chattahoochee River Bridge on Street Car Lane,
Atlanta-Marietta, Ga.

Canal Locks, Savannah River Initial Port of Augusta's Water Power, Augusta, Ga.

146

AUGUSTA, Ga. Steamer Loaded with Cotton at Wharf - Savannah River.

Savannah River.   AUGUSTA, Ga.

Steamer "John W. Callahan" Bainbridge, Ga.

Savannah-Atlanta Auto Route, Lane St., Brooklet, Ga.

"About twenty autos a week make the trip from Savannah to Atlanta,"
August 2, 1910

COLUMBUS, GA.   View on First Ave. showing parking system

14th St. Bridge, crossing Chattahoochee River, Columbus, Ga.

COLUMBUS, GA.   Boat Landing and Iron Works

SOUTHERN R.R.
Depot, Commerce, Ga.

Union Depot, Cordele, Ga.

I was here with Sparks Show, March 21-22nd 1909.

Unloaded on this track →

149

Darien Loading Platform, Altamaha River Transfer.
Dixie Highway.

RAPID TRANSIT,
DARIEN, GA.

Main Street West, Fort Valley, Ga.

Franklin Springs, (2 Miles from Royston, Ga.)

BISH AND HIS BULL GREENSBORO GA.
KELTON + FULLER
PHOTO

Union Station, Griffin, Ga.

5417 Ogeechee River Bridge near Guyton, Ga.

UNION DEPOT,
HELENA, GA.

ELECTRIC R·R. LOOKOUT MT

Arrival Street Car from Atlanta, Ga., Marietta, Ga.

A Mt. Airy Omnibus, Mt. Airy, Ga.

BENSON STREET, OXFORD, GA.

This is the way I travel wish you were here
to take a ride with me we would enjoy
our selves will go to Conyers to night—
So you see I am Tom May

AUTO-EQUIPMENT AT CENTRAL FIRE STATION.   ROME, GA.

Old Time Stern Wheel Boat "Alabama", Rome, Ga.

ST. MARYS & KINGSLAND R.R., ST. MARYS, GA.

The River Front and S. S. "City of Columbus", Savannah, Ga.

Tallulah Falls and Rabun Gap Railroad

T. F. + Rabun Gap Ry.

Georgia R. R. Station,
Thomson, Ga.

"Tift's Garage," Best Equipped in South Georgia, Tifton, Ga.

Rapid Transit, Washington, Ga.

South Atlantic Car Works, Waycross, Ga.

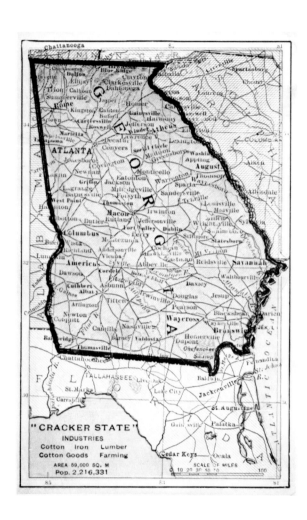

"CRACKER STATE"

INDUSTRIES

Cotton   Iron   Lumber
Cotton Goods   Farming

AREA 59,000 SQ. M
Pop. 2,216,331

W. L. Pierce, Purser, and Children at Browns Ferry,
near Hartwell, Ga., on the Blue Book High-Way.

INCLINE LOOKOUT MT.

LEISURE

*"I'm still enjoying myself, tho I find it
rather quiet while the men are out hunting."*

Then, as now, the mountains and the ocean attracted
Georgians on their summer vacations. They climbed onto
Umbrella Rock for the inevitable picture, hiked the mountain trails of North Georgia, and went to the beach at
Tybee Island. And there were other resorts that drew
them, like Indian Springs in Butts County and the grand
hotels in Thomasville. They walked Savannah's historic
squares and visited Providence Spring at Andersonville.

When they were not vacationing they found a great
deal to entertain them. In the cities there were the
parks, and Atlanta had a zoo that was as popular with

POOR ROBIN SPRING, NEAR OCMULGEE RIVER, AT ABBEVILLE, GA.

P. S. CLARK & CO.

DUSK HUNTING AROUND DARIEN, GA.   THE RESULT OF FINE SHOTS.

adults as with children. Movies were in their infancy, and the earliest motion picture theaters could be found only in the cities, but some of the larger towns had opera houses. Hunting was a popular sport for men, and every town had a baseball team and a well-worn diamond. Football was not the great spectator sport that it is today, but the games between college teams drew townspeople to the bleachers in the days before the building of stadiums.

There was boating and yachting, and bicycling, and a whole new crop of sports that came with the automobile, including endurance races. The racers roared through

Georgia's small towns, leaving a cloud of dust and an awe-struck crowd behind them. "I am in the 2nd auto from the right hand side. Bye Bye, Florence," wrote one of the senders on a card showing a Savannah Auto Club race as it passed through Covington.

Athens Cycle Company,
279 North Lumpkin, Athens, Ga.

White City Park, Atlanta, Ga.

AT THE ANIMAL PENS, GRANT PARK, ATLANTA, GA.

"Pure Ice Cream, High Grade Candies, Cigars and Tobacco"

V. D. L. CO.   30 MARIETTA STREET   ATLANTA, GA.

THE FASTEST AUTOMOBILE RACE COURSE IN THE WORLD

OPENING RACE MEETING NOVEMBER 9th TO 13th
ATLANTA AUTOMOBILE SPEEDWAY

William Knipper Driving a Chalmers-Detroit,
Atlanta Races, 1909

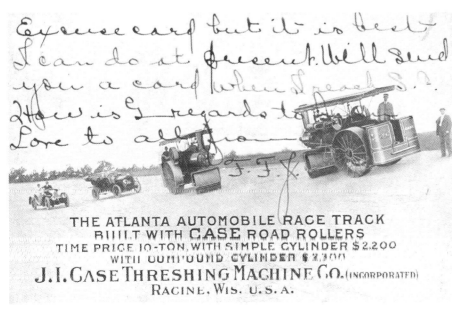

THE ATLANTA AUTOMOBILE RACE TRACK
BUILT WITH CASE ROAD ROLLERS
TIME PRICE 10-TON, WITH SIMPLE CYLINDER $2,200
WITH COMPOUND CYLINDER $2,300
J. I. CASE THRESHING MACHINE CO. (INCORPORATED)
RACINE, WIS. U.S.A.

162

Country Club, Summerville, near AUGUSTA, GA.

Dear Lund: This is the place the gentlemen of the party spend most of their time. Wish you — yours truly N.M.H.

My address is 317 Evans St.

A JOLLY AUTO PARTY, BAINBRIDGE, GA.

When did you hear from Dad?

Fishing on the Flint River, Bainbridge, Ga.

Yacht Racing, Brunswick, Ga.

Cloudland Park Club House.

INTERIOR COUNTRY CLUB, COLUMBUS, GA.

Savannah Auto Club Endurance Race
Passing, Covington, Ga.

I am in the auto from the right hand side. Bye Bye Florence 2/17/10.

Spring Park, Demorest, Ga.

Even if you have a face like
the one on the left
bring it to the
PUTNAM COUNTY FAIR
NOV. 15-19, EATONTON, GA.
and we will
send you
home with

one looking like this.

No cure, no pay.
Don't forget the date.

B-11   TALBOTT-ENO CO. DES MOINES

165

GRAND STAND – PUTNAM CO. FAIR, EATONTON, GA.

SWIFT LITHIA SPRINGS
ELBERTON, GA.

BIRD HUNTING, NEAR FITZGERALD, GA.

A good Day's Work, Fort Screven, Ga.

Lover's Leap, Franklin, Ga. Made during Sun's Eclipse, June 28, 1908.

State Day 1913, Gainesville, Ga.

Our car on State day

Mineral Springs, Graymont, Ga.

Views of Mineral Springs, Graymont, Ga.

Hawkinsville Chautauqua.   1909.

Jekyll Island, Ga.

Raymond, Walter, and Gordon Sanford
Viewing Northwest Georgia
from Umbrella Rock on Lookout
Mountain, circa 1920

Club House, near Millen, Ga.

Chas Hill Reed
Ormsic Georgia

Supplied by the famous WARM SPRINGS flowing 1800 Gallons per minute

NEW WARM SPRINGS POOL

On Pine Mountain elevation 1200 ft.

Georgia Warm Springs

Temperature of water 90% Winter and Summer
THE SOUTHS GREATEST NATATORIUM
10000 sq. feet Swimming Space - Holds 450000 Gals of water

Firemen's Parade, Rome, Ga

COUNTRY CLUB, ROME, GA.
1379

Savannah Grand Prize and Vanderbilt Cup Race 1911
Auto Course at Hayners Bridge.

Edwin Bergdoll Driving a Benz,
Savannah Races, probably 1911

YACHT CLUB HOUSE, NEAR SAVANNAH, GA.

Savannah Yacht Club, Savannah, Ga.

WILLINGHAM'S COTTAGE CAMP

25 Miles South of Savannah (On Atlantic Coastal Highway) 130 Miles North of Jacksonville

Roasting Oysters, a Popular Pastime Around Savannah, Ga.

Casino Thunderboldt, Near Savannah, Ga.

New Hotel Tybee and Beach,
Tybee Island, near Savannah, Ga.

Bathing Scene, Tybee, Ga.

CLUB HOUSE OF OCEAN POND HUNTING AND FISHING CLUB NEAR VALDOSTA, GA.

White Sulphur Springs House, White Sulphur Springs, Ga.

Street Scene, Chauncey, Ga.

Georgia and Herbert Looking Down
750 ft. from Devils' Pulpit
1907
Tallulah Falls, Ga.

Motor Car on Tallulah Falls R. R.,
Tallulah Falls, Ga.

HOTELS

"I guess we have found the place at last—
a fine hotel $6 per week, a piano in the parlor."

Many of the hotels that made their way onto picture post cards were impressive structures—indeed, designed to impress—with their high-ceilinged lobbies and sweeping galleries. They were planned for families, and families were larger then, sometimes including five or more children, but also unmarried aunts and uncles in addition to grandparents. The guests therefore required, not a room, but rooms, and in the resort hotels—which some of these were—the guests' stays were frequently long ones.

A familial relationship existed between the hotel and its guests, so that those who made it a custom to spend late summer at, say, the Mitchell House in Thomasville or the Lithia Hotel at Tallapoosa often met families they had

The Georgian Terrace Hotel and The Ponce de Leon Apartments, Atlanta, Ga.

HOTEL COMER, COMER, GA.

come to know there summers earlier. They often reserved the same rooms, season to season. Sociability was in fact one of the things that these homes away from home offered—the opportunity to visit in the lobby and to rock, and talk, on the galleries. Another was the luxury of a reserved table in the dining room, where a splendid meal awaited. Hotel dining rooms, like railroad dining cars, were legendary for their bounty.

There were smaller, less elegant hotels, many of these also seen on the post cards. They catered to traveling salesmen and other overnight guests, although there were often a few local business people who occupied permanent rooms there. The more common custom was for

those individuals to take rooms in private residences. And there were the boardinghouses—private homes whose owners had converted them into hotels of a sort, where one could rent a room (usually with bath down the hall) and take one's meals at the boardinghouse table. As automobile travel increased, some opened their homes to the travelers as "tourist homes," forerunners of the Days Inns and Ramadas.

GUESTS AT WIGWAM HOTEL, INDIAN SPRINGS, GA.

The Monarch Hotel, Tallapoosa, Ga.

177

WINDSOR HOTEL, AMERICUS, GA.

LADIES LOUNGE.   HOTEL GEORGIAN, ATHENS, GA.   COFFEE SHOP.

LOBBY, HOTEL ANSLEY, ATLANTA, GA.

The New Kimball House, Atlanta, Ga.

AUGUSTA, Ga. Planters Hotel. *Do you remember this*

Hotel, Main Street, Austell, Ga.

PARK HOTEL.
CARTERSVILLE. GA

House
100 years old

1906

BLUE RIDGE HOTEL

Hotel Annex

5363 Blue Ridge Hotel. Altitude 2250 ft., Clayton, Ga. W. T. Dozier. Mngr

Commercial Hotel, Cornelia, Ga.

180

Gay Hotel, Cuthbert, Ga.

Dawson Inn, Dawson, Ga.

OCONEE SPRINGS HOTEL, NEAR EATONTON, GA.

HOTEL ROBERTS. ELBERTON, GA.

Lee-Grant Hotel, Fitzgerald, Ga.

Winona Hotel, Fort Valley, Ga.

Hotel Albert, Graymont, Ga.

5416 Central Hotel, Guyton, Ga.

Pierce Hotel, Hazlehurst, Ga. Pub. by W. T. Patrick, Hazlehurst, Ga.

183

Partial View of Lobby, Wigwam Hotel, Indian Springs, Ga.

8074

HOTEL ELDER, INDIAN SPRING GA.

Hotel Miona, Miona Springs, Ga.

The Walton Hotel, Monroe, Ga.

HOTEL COLQUITT. Moultrie, Ga.

Olympia Hotel, Newnan, Ga.
Presented by Newnan Restaurant Co.

Parker House,
Nicholls, Ga.

BS30B2

Saint Elmo Hotel.
Pub. for T. E. Culbreath's Drug Store, Palmetto, Ga

Marble Hill Hotel, Rockmart, Ga.

ST. MARY'S HOUSE, ST. MARYS, GA.

De Soto Hotel, Savannah, Ga

Lithia Hotel, Tallapoosa, Ga.

Cliff House, Tallulah Falls, Ga.

GLENBROOK,   TALLULAH FALLS, GA

MURRAY HOTEL
Thomaston, Ga.

This is where I stop. M.C.M. 12/13/06

188

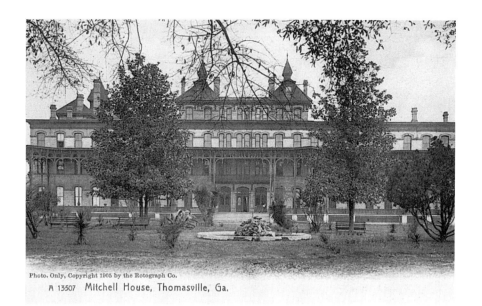

Photo. Only, Copyright 1905 by the Rotograph Co.

A 13507 Mitchell House, Thomasville, Ga.

Trion Inn, Trion Ga.

No. 9054. Hotel Tybee, Tybee Island, Ga.

Colonial Hotel, Vidalia, Ga.   18558

LaGrande Hotel, Waycross, Ga.

Dining
Room Hotel
Charles,
West Point,
Ga.

Bed Room, White Sulphur Springs Hotel

Hotel Winecoff.
Atlanta, Ga.

ZIMMER'S MOUNTAIN LODGE, Dahlonega, Ga.

Much of the rich history of Dahlonega, Ga., is preserved in this rustic fireplace in the lobby of the Mountain Lodge. It is made of Gold, Copper, Garnet, Quartz and other ores taken from the surrounding mountains.

THE SOLDIER'S LIFE

"It is fine to be a real soldier.
Your friend, Priv. Beatty Torbett."

The views of army camps that appear on post cards from the early 1900s are reminders of the 1898 war with Spain that had been fought over a period of only a few months in the Philippines and in Cuba. But there seems to be an air of ease about the peacetime soldiers posed on the gallery of the building at Fort McPherson near Atlanta. None yet foresees the war that was to engulf Europe in 1914 and that the United States would enter three years later. With the coming of the war, training camps such as Camp Gordon at Chamblee and Camp Wheeler in Macon were established, and thousands of young men from

VIEW OF CAMP BARKER ON ST. SIMONS ISLAND WITH ST. SIMONS LIGHTHOUSE IN DISTANCE.   Photo by Silverstein of Savannah.

Greetings from Nat'l. Y. W. C. A., Camp Gordon, Ga. Hostess House

Georgia and other states got their training here as well as at the older camps such as Fort Oglethorpe in northwest Georgia. Trench warfare in France dictated that the training include not only marching and ten-mile hikes but gunnery and bayonet practice.

The presence of the camps also brought the war closer to home to the people who lived in nearby communities and who cheered the men when they marched through the streets to the trains that would carry them to their points of embarkation. The war of 1917–18 was deadly serious business. Only 236 of the original 591 men who made up the 151st Machine Gun Battalion, a part of the famed Rainbow Division, returned home to Macon. Other towns and cities across the state counted their losses. The Armistice ended the fighting and became a national day of remembrance.

Camp Wheeler, Ga.

Photo House, Official Photog. U. S. Gov.

STREET SCENE.

PASSED BY CENSOR, WASHINGTON, D. C. © I. F. S.

ON A TEN MILE HIKE, CAMP GORDON, ATLANTA, GA.   222829

Greetings from Nat'l Y. W. C. A., Camp Gordon, Ga Hostess House

FIELD HOSPITAL. CAMP HANCOCK. AUGUSTA. GA.

MOTOR TRUCKS, CAMP HANCOCK, AUGUSTA, GA.

LIBERTY THEATRE. CAMP HANCOCK. GA.

ARTILLERY SECTION, CAMP HANCOCK, AUGUSTA, GA.

Fort McPherson, Ga.

GERMAN PRISONERS BUILDING PRISON CAMP. FORT McPHERSON, GA.

HEADQUARTERS, FT. McPHERSON, GA.

Fort McPherson, Ga.

Receiving a Dispatch at Field Headquarters,
Fort Oglethorpe, Ga.

Fort Oglethorpe, Ga.

Field Day Jousting Contest,
Fort Oglethorpe, Ga.

Fort Oglethorpe, Ga.

DADY'S HOUSE

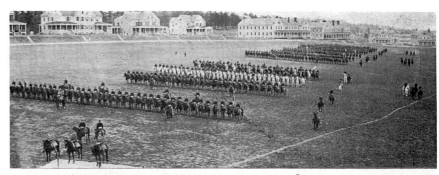

The Gallant 12th at Fort Oglethorpe, Ga.

L. A. W. NOVELTY CO., PUB., SPRINGFIELD. MASS.

Dec 7th

Dear Mother, I have not forgotten that
I owe you a letter and will try and
write it soon. We are all well.
Love to all.   J Hasser.

ONE OF THE Y. M. C. A. BLDGS, Camp at Fort Oglethorpe and Chickamauga Park, Ga

No. 4, 8 inch, Fort Screven, Ga.

Changing Sentinels,
Fort Screven, Ga.

Bird's Eye View Fort Screven. Tybee Island near Savannah, Ga.

Company F, Fort Screven, Ga.

Camp Wheeler, Ga.

ReMEMBERING THE PAST

"The reunions at your house were always so pleasant."

One of the things the early post cards tell us about the photographers who took these pictures—and ultimately about the people who bought the cards and mailed them—is that they had a sense of history. Otherwise there would not be as many views as there are of subjects such as the oldest grocery store or the town's first post office. Nor would there be so many views of reunions of Confederate veterans. The cards of course date from a time when the Civil War was no more than forty or fifty years in the past—as recent to those living in the early 1900s as World War II is to us now. Indeed, there were still a great many living reminders of that war, and towns and cities across the South erected monuments to them.

Atlanta, Ga.

The homes of wartime governor Joseph E. Brown and Confederate Secretary of State Robert Toombs were shrines of a sort—as was the room in Washington, Georgia, where the president of the Confederacy, fleeing south from Richmond, held his last cabinet meeting. Georgians also remembered a Union general named Sherman and his march from Atlanta to Savannah, and commemorated his visit with views like the one of a house in Marietta that he used as a signal station. The National Cemetery at Andersonville recalled the prison where thirteen thousand Union prisoners died in slightly more than a year, and veterans of the Union army visited the spring—Providence Spring, they called it—that had

providentially supplied them with fresh drinking water.

The slave cabins at the Hermitage and elsewhere in the state provided memories of a different sort. But it was the "big house," the Hermitage itself and houses like it, that shaped the popular vision of what life before the war had been like and that fed the imagination of a young Georgia woman named Margaret Mitchell.

The Marshes of Glynn and Laniers Oak, Brunswick, Ga.

The Hermitage, Savannah, Ga.

Savannah, Ga. Mansion of the Hermitage.

VIEW IN NATIONAL CEMETERY, ANDERSONVILLE, GA.

Published by Souvenir Art Co.

Locomotive General,

The Historic Engine "TEXAS."
Used by Captain William A Fuller in the pursuit and capture
of the "GENERAL" and the Andrews Raiders on April 12, 1862.

First Post Office of Atlanta, Ga.

Copyright 1911—Witt Bros.

"Uncle Remus and Home,
Atlanta, Ga.

Stone Mountain.
The Largest Solid Stone in the World.
Picture taken near the Mountain.
Atlanta, Ga.

Sutherland, Home of Gen. John B. Gordon, Confederate Leader and
Southern Orator, Near Atlanta, Ga.

OLDEST BUILDING IN ATLANTA, GA.

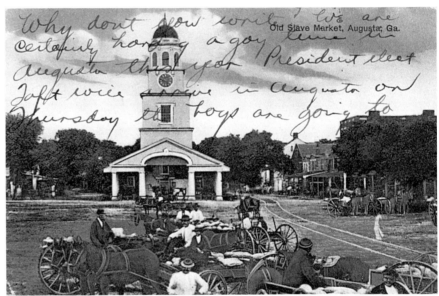

Old Slave Market, Augusta, Ga.

Why don't you write? We are certainly having a gay time in Augusta this year. President elect Taft will arrive in Augusta on Thursday the boys are going to

15101—
Meadow Garden
Washington
Headquarters
when near
Augusta, Ga.

Birth Place of Ty Cobb, Born in Banks County,
Georgia, Dec. 18th, 1886.
Copyright, 1911, by John J. Rampley, Carnesville, Ga.

House where Judge Logan E. Blakely spent his boyhood days near Clayton, Ga. An Old
Time Georgia Scene.

PUB. BY GEORGE W. HORAN, DALTON, GA.

Unveiling of the
Confederate
Monument.
La Grange, Ga.

CHEHAW MONUMENT NEAR LEESBURG, GA.
ERECTED BY COUNCIL OF SAFETY CHAPTER DAR
AMERICUS, GA.   UNVEILED JUNE 14, 1912.

Old Slave Market, Built in 1758, Louisville, Ga.

Sidney Lanier's Birthplace, Macon, Ga.

United Sons of Confederate Veterans Reunion, May 7-8-9, 1912.

Gate to Central City Park, Macon, Ga.
General John B. Gordon Camp.
United Confederate Veterans Reunion. May 7-8-9, 1912.

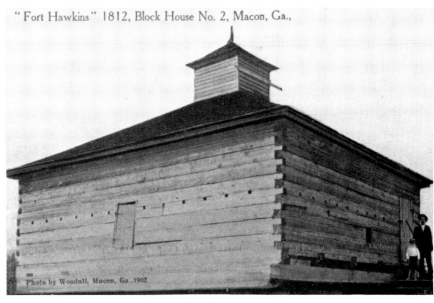

"Fort Hawkins" 1812, Block House No. 2, Macon, Ga.,

Photo by Woodall, Macon, Ga., 1902

209

G. A. R. Parade during Convention,
April, 1912, Marietta, Ga.

House used by Sherman as Signal Station during War of Rebellion on Campbell's Hill, Marietta, Ga.

MIDWAY. AN OLD REVOLUTIONARY CHURCH AND CEMETERY. LIBERTY COUNTY, GA.
Midway bet'ween Savannah and Darien, Ga., on the Dixie and Quebec-Miami Highway.

210

The Old Capitol of Ga. Erected in 1806. Now Georgia Military College.

Bullock Home, near Atlanta, where mother of President Roosevelt was raised

Bonaventure Cemetery, near SAVANNAH, Ga.

Do you think I must be hard up for a card, to send you one of a cemetery? No, but it is a beautiful place, reminds me of the one in Athens.

Slave Cabins,
The Hermitage, Savannah, Ga.

HERMITAGE SAVANNAH GA.

General Sherman's Headquarters. SAVANNAH, Ga.

Having a fine time. It is so hot. Ella

Colonial Park, First Burial Ground in Savannah, Ga

"The Old Dominion," Sparta, Ga.
The First Georgia Methodist Conference
was held here in 1806.

TYBEE ROADS, MARTELLO TOWER, TYBEE ISLAND, GA.　　E. C. KROPP CO. PUBL. MILWAUKEE. NO. 3607

213

SLATON-GREEN DRUG CO.
LAST CABINET MEETING PLACE OF CONFEDERACY, WASHINGTON, GA.

HAND-COLORED

SLATON-GREEN DRUG CO.
ROOM WHERE LAST CONFEDERATE CABINET MEETING WAS HELD, WASHINGTON, GA.

With best wishes for a Merry Xmas
Lucile Norman

GEN. ROBT. TOOMBS' RESIDENCE, WASHINGTON, GA.

I got home all right Will see you Monday

Providence Spring,
Andersonville, Ga.

Grady Monument, Atlanta, Ga.

WELCOME U. C. V.!
TWENTY-NINTH ANNUAL REUNION.
UNITED CONFEDERATE VETERANS.
ATLANTA, GA., OCTOBER 7 TO 11 1919
Above composite picture including actual aerial photograph of Atlanta, designed and
copyrighted by The Atlanta Journal Staff Photographers.

215

Scene where Jefferson Davis was captured in 1865, near Fitzgerald, Ga.

Gen. Wm. McIntosh

McIntosh Rock

INDIAN SPRINGS, GA.

FIRST MONUMENT ERECTED TO THE CONFEDERATE DEAD, STONEWALL CEMETERY, GRIFFIN, GA.

HAND-COLORED

This Tree Marks Spot Where Dr. Crawford W. Long First.
Discovered Anaesthesia, March 30th, 1842 at Jefferson, Ga.,
Jackson County.

THE ORIGINAL CABIN
MOUNT BERRY, GA

Old Time Loom. An Old Time Georgia Scene.

INDEX TO COUNTIES

INDEX TO TOWNS